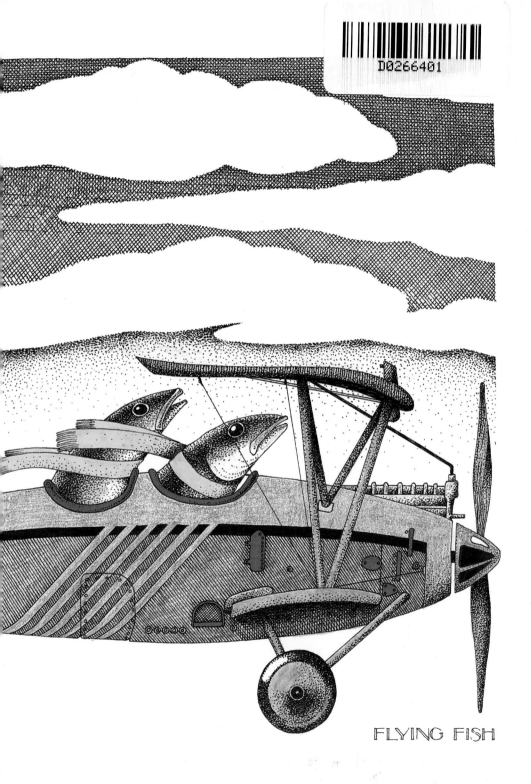

FLYING FISH

Drake playing with bowls.

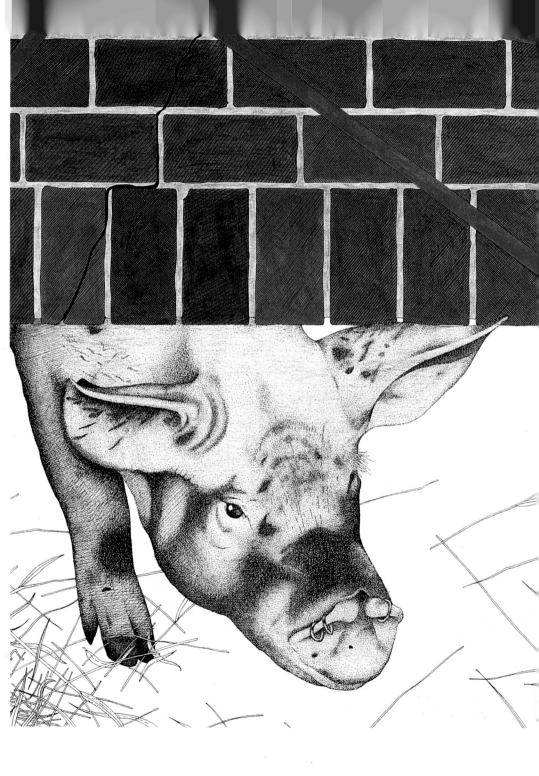

Still Warthogs Run Deep

and other free range nonsense

Drawings
and Verses
by
Simon Drew

ANTIQUE COLLECTORS' CLUB

MOLE OF KINTYRE

to Caroline
and her parents, who know what a lot of
nonsense is talked about farming,
and to Sue K

© 1988 Simon Drew
World copyright reserved
First published 1988
Reprinted 1990
ISBN 1 85149 087 6

British Library CIP data
Drew, Simon
    Still warthogs run deep and other free
range nonsense.
    I. Title II. Antique Collectors' Club
821'.914

Published and printed in England by the Antique Collectors' Club Ltd.,
Woodbridge, Suffolk.

4

Contents :

geese in our time

THE WILD GOOSE CHASE

A story has just come to light
concerning one man's chase :
     his famous goose
      was running loose
and he was in disgrace.

The goose had been a well known sight
performing cunning tricks :
     it seemed to know
      where truffles grow
and how to count to six.

And so you see this farmer's plight :
the goose could make him rich
     or failing that
      could make him fat.
He didn't care much which.

A record of this feathered flight
was made at every stage
     and one such bird
      (though well interred)
appeared on every page.

It all began one day at tea:
the saga's seeds were sown.
    A passing nun
    remarked: "my son,
I think your bird has flown."

Inspection proved the bird was free.
The farmer's task was clear:
    he needed bait
    so fetched a crate
of freshly bottled beer.

He knew the lure of ale would bring
it running from its hide
    and so he bore
    his bitter store
around the countryside.

He tied a length of coloured string
around each bottle's neck
    and dragged it round
    along the ground
and carried on his trek.

Between two wooded mountain sides
he found a river mouth.
A dog-eared priest
was facing east;
his dog was facing south.

"I've never seen your goose, besides
you didn't say hello,"
the priest replied,
"but have you tried
my organist; he'll know."

And so the farmer thanked him well
and stepped inside the church,
and asked the gent
of tuneful bent
how he could help the search.

"I know three brothers, strange to tell,
who run a home for geese.
I'll show you soon,
but first a tune:
I'll play my party piece."

The organist could not be stopped:
he played as though possessed.
        The farmer slept
        then woke and crept
away and missed the rest.

He walked until he nearly dropped
along the windswept coast
        past lakes and hills
        and daffodils
(of which he saw a host).

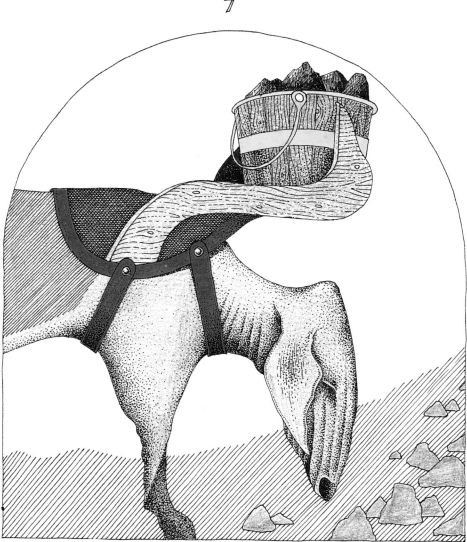

A sleeping beast he came across
looked slightly like a goat;
    it hardly woke
    despite a yoke
secured around its throat.

When questioned it became quite cross;
though clearly not impressed,
    he felt it would
    have understood
and could have helped his quest.

But in the end he found the place,
the brothers' home for strays.
His smiling face
revealed his chase
could start its final phase.

"Has anybody seen a trace,
I really need to know?
You see, my goose
is running loose."
The brother answered: "No."

The second brother came indoors,
a man way past his youth.
   "Excuse me Sir,
    would you prefer
to let me know the truth ?"

"Though hares have ears and cats have paws
and bloodhounds eyes look sad,
   the Golden Gate
   is silver plate."
The man was raving mad.

"I'm sure you're hiding something here,"
he bellowed at the third.
        "Please, be my guide,"
            the farmer sighed,
"and help me find my bird."

"Just help yourself; there's nothing queer
and take no heed of him.
        To our dismay
            some people say
they think our brother's grim."

The farmer now could scour the place:
the goose pens for a start.
        With fine toothed comb
        he searched their home
by tearing it apart.

He looked in every jar and case
and emptied every drawer,
        and rifled through
        their clothing too,
though goodness knows what for.

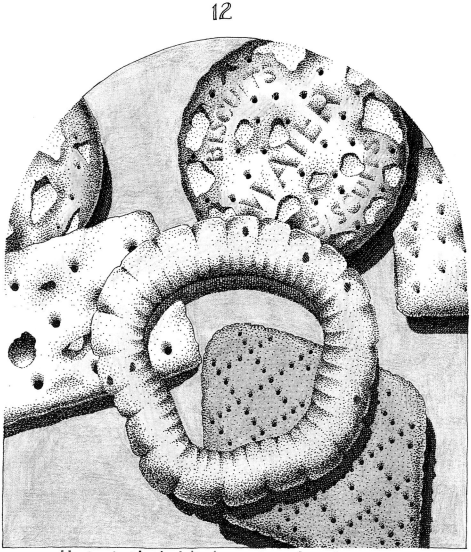

He took their kitchen store by storm,
threw biscuits all around,
    with shredded wheat
    around his feet
you couldn't see the ground.

He thought he should be getting warm,
but still the goose was lost:
    so persevered
    until he feared
he couldn't bear the cost.

So having looked through fields and trees
and opened every door,
    he hung his head:
    the trail was dead.
He said he'd search no more.

And after lunch of pie and peas
he waved a tired goodbye.
    I think somehow
    he knows by now
the contents of that pie.

pig on head
epidemic
spreads

a scene with a herd....

scene but not herd

SHEEP
DIP

25

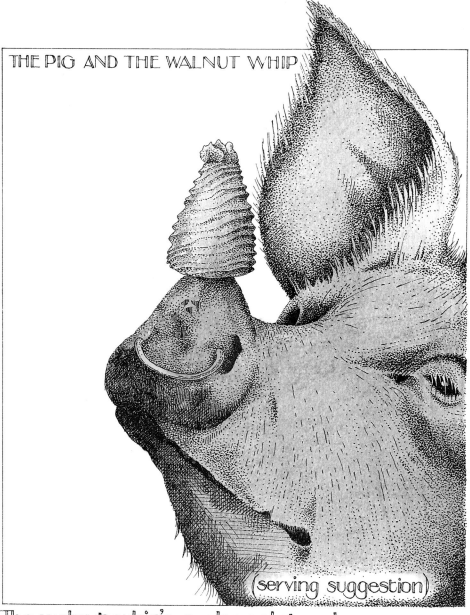

(serving suggestion)

The walnut whip's a chocolate dream:
Its taste is so elusive.
It's whipped and whisked and hurled around
to make a whirled exclusive.

26

SHEEPWRECK

....and all I ask is a tall sheep....
....and a star to steer her by.

DOUBLE GRAZING

THE SKATEGOAT

when did you last see your farmer?

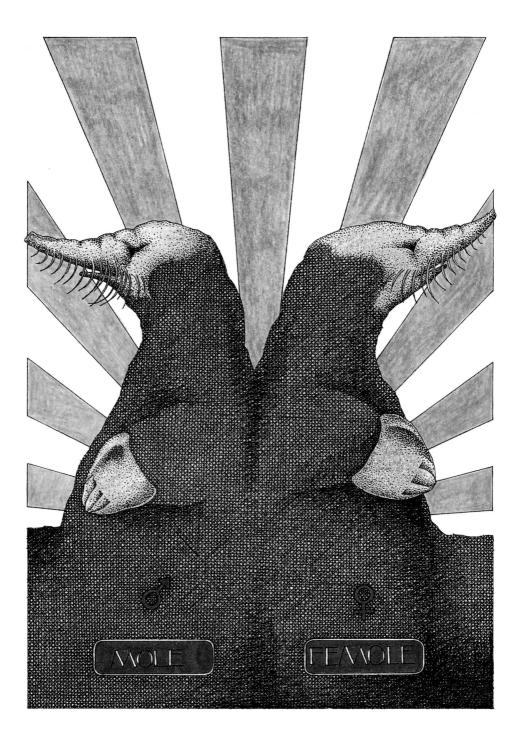

BURNING THE CAMEL
AT BOTH ENDS

Last Christmas........

Aunt Agatha gave me a piglet ,
that winds up and runs round the floor:
its movement is so realistic
that I think it's a bit of a boar.

An Unlikely Story

Somewhere left of Everest
there lived a worried shepherd:
    the sheep he'd reared
    had disappeared.
He tried to blame a leopard.

But then the monster struck again
and ate a native porter;
    the people cried
    at one so wide
that spouted jets of water.

And though a footprint had been made
with something like a flipper,
    Tibetan tales
    discounted whales
and called it Yak the Ripper.

.... there lived a worried shepherd.....

While walking through some farmyard pens,
past ploughs with rusty blades,

amongst the turkeys, geese and hens,
he found the three of spades.

The Six Foot Duck

Very few have seen
this distinctive breed of bird;
it was reared on royal farms
when required by George the Third.
But what the king desired
when he made the regal wish
was a duck with four more legs
for his next majestic dish.
For when the chance arose
he ate drumsticks by the score
and the six foot duck he meant
would produce an extra four.
So now the end result
of this misconstrued request
is a lanky useless bird
that can build a six foot nest.

a farmer whose wheat never grew
crossed a cow with a red kangaroo:
the offspring they say
gave milkshakes all day
and more than enough oxtail stew.

A farmer of wealth who was frightened of pigs
decided to put them on diets:
he fed them on buckets of syrup of figs
but they answered his kindness with riots.
    And though he thought it really should
    it didn't seem to do them good

A farmer of wealth was so frightened of sheep
he'd worry about them for hours :
because his forebodings were losing him sleep
he tried to win favour with flowers.
       And though he thought it really should
       it didn't seem to do them good.

A farmer of wealth who was frightened of cows
would hide in his barn to avoid them:
he'd find any reason to get out of rows
and never did things that annoyed them.
  And though he thought it really should
  it didn't seem to do them good.

This farmer of wealth was so nervous and stressed
he always seemed ready to panic:
his doctors suggested he needed a rest
with a trip on the S.S. Titanic.
     And though he thought it really should
     it didn't seem to do him good.

THOSE DARK SATANIC MOLES